Life in Colonial America

Linda R. Wade

Visit us at
www.abdopub.com

Published by ABDO Publishing Company, 4940 Viking Drive, Edina, MN 55435.
Copyright ©2001 by Abdo Consulting Group, Inc. International copyrights
reserved in all countries. No part of this book may be reproduced in any form
without written permission from the publisher.

Printed in the United States.

Contributing Editor: John Hamilton
Graphic Design, Illustrations: John Hamilton
Cover photo: Corbis
Interior photos: Corbis

Sources: Kalman, Bobbie. *The Early Family Home.* New York: Crabtree
Publishing Company, 1982; Kalman, Bobbie. *Early Settler Children.* New
York: Crabtree Publishing Company, 1982; Kalman, Bobbie. *Early Travel.*
New York: Crabtree Publishing Company, 1981; Kalman, Bobbie. *Food For
the Settler.* New York: Crabtree Publishing Company, 1982; Kalman, Bobbie.
Historic Communities: Colonial Life. New York: Crabtree Publishing
Company, 1992; Kent, Deborah. *America the Beautiful: Connecticut.* Chicago:
Childrens Press, 1990; Kent, Deborah. *America the Beautiful: Massachusetts.*
Chicago: Childrens Press, 1987; McGovern, Ann. *If You Lived in Colonial
Times.* New York: Scholastic Book Service, 1964; McNair, Sylvia. *America the
Beautiful: New Hampshire.* Chicago: Childrens Press, 1992; McNair, Sylvia.
America the Beautiful: Virginia. Chicago: Childrens Press, 1989; Scott, John
Anthony. *The Story of America.* Washington, D.C.: National Geographic
Society, 1984; Tunis, Edwin. *Colonial Living.* New York: Thomas Y. Crowell
Company, 1957; World Book Encyclopedia, 1990; Zeman, Anne. *Everything
You Need to Know About American History Homework.* New York: Scholastic
Reference, 1994.

Library of Congress Cataloging–in–Publication Data

Wade, Linda R.
    Life in Colonial America / Linda R. Wade
        p. cm. -- (The American Revolution)
    Includes index.
    ISBN 1-57765-152-9
    1. United States -- Social life and customs -- To 1775 -- Juvenile literature. [1.
United States -- Social life and customs -- To 1775.] I. Title.
    E188 .W215 2000
    973 -- dc21
                                                    00--059411

CONTENTS

INTRODUCTION

The first settlers came to America in sailing ships from various European countries. They came for different reasons. Some were explorers. Others were seeking riches and adventure. The Pilgrims came so they could have religious freedom. All were seeking a new life in the New World.

Most of these settlers were men. However, in time women came to marry the men who were living in the New World. These people faced unknown hazards and death, as well as success.

As more and more people came to America, simple settlements became known as the Colonies. These were grouped by location: the New England, Middle, and Southern Colonies. Life was different in each area.

Above: The landing of the Pilgrims at Plymouth, Massachusetts, December 22, 1620. *Facing page:* Costumed actors in Colonial Williamsburg, Virginia.

CHAPTER 1

THE NEW ENGLAND COLONIES

The New England Colonies were often called the Northern Colonies because they were the northern-most states. New Hampshire, Massachusetts, Rhode Island, and Connecticut made up the New England Colonies (Maine at that time was a part of Massachusetts). People who lived along the Atlantic coast in this area were often fishermen and whalers. Many had jobs in the shipping industry. In fact, Massachusetts had become the center of shipbuilding.

People who lived inland were often employed as loggers, since trees covered the land. Many were craftsmen, making cabinets and tables out of wood.

Another occupation of the New Englanders was fur trading. They trapped animals, and sold or traded their hides. Pelts from beaver, mink, raccoon, muskrat, and rabbit were in demand both in the Colonies and in England.

Since the weather was colder in the north, farms were small. They planted corn, rye, oats, barley, peas, squash, onions, and turnips. Corn had been the staple crop since the days of the Pilgrims.

The Massachusetts towns of Salem and Boston were the main seaports. Ships brought supplies from the other Colonies through these ports.

CHAPTER 2

THE MIDDLE COLONIES

The Middle Colonies consisted of New York, New Jersey, Delaware, and Pennsylvania. They were located between the New England and Southern Colonies. Many farms were found here. Wheat, rye, oats, and barley were the main crops.

The Middle Colonies had the most industry. They manufactured products needed in the other areas, including glass, leather goods, shoes, and barrels. They also made guns, axes, and tools. New York City and Philadelphia became the main Atlantic ports.

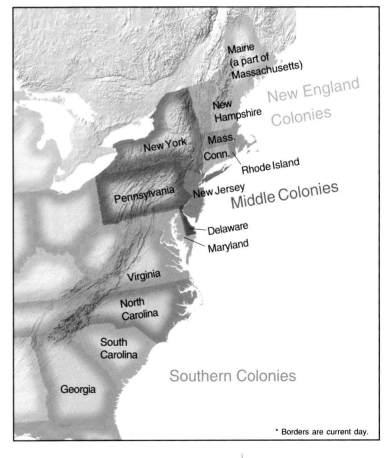

Maine
(a part of Massachusetts)

New Hampshire

New England Colonies

New York

Mass.

Conn.

Rhode Island

Pennsylvania

New Jersey

Middle Colonies

Delaware

Maryland

Virginia

North Carolina

South Carolina

Southern Colonies

Georgia

* Borders are current day.

CHAPTER 3

THE SOUTHERN COLONIES

Virginia was the first colony established by the British. It was a Southern Colony. Maryland, North Carolina, South Carolina, and Georgia were also Southern Colonies. The largest farms were located here. The warm climate and mineral-rich soil grew abundant crops of cotton, sugarcane, tobacco, rice, and indigo. Indigo was an important plant to the colonists because it made a deep blue dye, which was put into large vats. Cotton and wool cloth was then added to color the material.

The heavily landscaped garden outside the mansion at the Boone Hall Plantation, Charleston, South Carolina.

An actor playing a slave walks past a farmhouse.

The Southern Colonies had a big market for their products. Cloth and tobacco were wanted throughout Europe. They had markets with the other Colonies, but they exported many of their goods to England and other European countries. The demand was great.

As a result, some farms became very large and were then called plantations. Slaves were often purchased by the landowners. Often the slaves worked in the fields from early morning to sundown. Most masters were mean to their slaves. Sometimes they split the families. Sometimes they beat the slaves.

The landowner built the main house. Behind this primary building was the kitchen, smokehouse, beach house, and barn. The cabins, where the slaves lived, were also behind the main house. Charleston, South Carolina and Savannah, Georgia, were the primary southern ports on the Atlantic coast.

CHAPTER 4

LIFE IN THE VILLAGES

All the villages had certain people who helped everyone. The village blacksmith was one of these people. He was a skilled craftsman. In his shop, he heated metal until it was red hot, then used an anvil to shape the metal into whatever was needed. When it was formed correctly, he dipped the item into cold water. Sometimes he had to do this several times to temper the steel.

Horseshoes were one of the most essential things the blacksmith made. They were used to protect the feet of horses. Blacksmiths also made nails to help the colonists build their homes and barns. Hinges, latches, and farm tools were available for purchase in this shop.

A blacksmith uses a hammer and spike to ridge and pierce holes in a red-hot horseshoe.

A man in historical costume outside the post office of Colonial Williamsburg, Virginia.

The post office was a common meeting place. The postmaster knew all the members of the community. He handed mail out to the residents when they came in. For the smaller communities, a post rider carried mail from farm to farm. He had designated points where he changed horses.

Sometimes there was a butcher shop, where animals were killed and packaged. Hams and slabs of bacon were hung in the smokehouse to cure. The smokehouse was a little building where meat was hung. A fire using hickory wood burned for several days and made the meat tasty. The butcher made sausage, which was also smoked. Meat either had to be smoked or canned to keep it from spoiling.

One of the best customers for the butcher was the shoemaker. He bought the hides and made all sorts of leather products, including shoes and boots. Butchering was usually done in the autumn on the farm, but animals were killed in the butcher shop any time of the year.

The editor of the local newspaper made a point of knowing everything about everyone. Social events were always of interest to the people. Often visitors would be named. Notices of the sales of goods and property kept the conversations in the general store lively. Political news was usually several months old by the time it was printed. Of course, deaths, births, and weddings were described in great detail.

The newspaper was small, usually only four pages. It took a long time to make because all the type had to be set by hand. The editor also made signs for people.

A town crier.

Some villages had a town crier. He sang out the latest news at each corner. He also made public announcements. He was especially important to villages where there was no newspaper.

Other important people in the village included the broom maker, who made brooms from the stalks of various grains that were bound tightly by a wire band. Another shop found in a village was that of the weaver. He made rugs for the colonists. The miller was a necessary person. Farmers took bags of wheat and corn to the miller, who ground it into flour and cornmeal. These two items were necessary for making bread, biscuits, and cornbread, three staples for the meals of the colonists.

Most shops had an apprentice. This was a person who was learning how to do the work of the business. If he worked in the blacksmith shop, he learned how to make metal hot enough to forge the needed article and then to pound it into shape.

The town surveyor was an important person. He charted the wilderness and laid out plots of ground for the farmers.

Since many of the Colonies were formed to provide religious freedom, the place chosen for the church was a major concern. Most

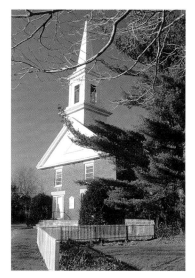

An old Colonial church in Harrisville, New Hampshire.

villages had at least one church. Sometimes it also served as a general meeting house. It could even become the courtroom, especially if the general store was very busy. The preacher, or parson as he was sometimes called, frequently traveled from village to village on a circuit. Young people who wanted to get married planned the date around the time when the preacher would arrive.

Lawyers and judges also traveled on a circuit. Trials were set according to the expected arrival date of the judge. These trials frequently took place in the general store.

The general store was often found in the center of the village. There was always a good smell in the store like cinnamon or coffee or any number of spices. It was one of the social centers of the village. Here people gathered to talk about the news. They shared their daily schedules and made community decisions. Gardens and crops were always a topic for discussion.

Sometimes the people traded seeds with each other. They also traded with the storekeeper. Items like eggs and butter might be exchanged for cloth, sugar, molasses, spices, coffee, rice, glassware, or gunpowder. Children loved to go to the general store for rock candy, a hard and very sweet type of candy.

Right: Merchandise is neatly stacked on the shelves of an old general store.

13

CHAPTER 5

COLONIAL SCHOOLS

Another important place in the village was the schoolhouse. It was usually located at the edge of town. All the children went to the same school. They were all in one room. This is why their schools were called one-room schoolhouses. The teacher would give each grade an assignment. Then, in turn, the different grades went to the front to recite their lessons. They frequently learned their spelling words and arithmetic facts by repeating them out loud. Sometimes it was a noisy place. There were three main subjects, including reading, writing, and arithmetic (called math today).

The inside of a one-room schoolhouse.

The one-room schoolhouse was often located at the edge of the village.

If the teacher was a man, he was called a schoolmaster. If the teacher was a woman, she was called a schoolmistress. The teacher often lived at the back of the schoolhouse or next door. Sometimes the teacher lived in the homes of students. Discipline was very strict. The schoolmaster might crack fingers with a stick for punishment, or put the student in a corner with a dunce cap on his head. Sometimes he even spanked pupils who misbehaved.

Paper was scarce. Students usually had slate boards. These were little blackboards that the children could hold. The schoolmaster would give them a problem, which they would work on. As soon as the schoolmaster saw the correct answer on the slate it could be wiped clean. Sometimes they used this slate board to write words down. As soon as the child memorized a spelling, the slate would be cleaned again.

The schoolmaster or schoolmistress helped children learn the "3 R's" (reading, writing, and arithmetic).

Students also used a hornbook, which was a wooden paddle that had an attached piece of paper. On the paper, the alphabet and numbers were written down to help the students. Sometimes a Bible verse or prayer was also written.

School was held only when it was convenient to the farming season, since most children had to help in the fields. School would begin after the crops were in and end when planting began. Girls seldom went to school past the sixth grade. Boys stayed through the eighth grade. A few were able to go to college.

All the children helped keep the school clean and warm. Boys carried wood in from outside. The girls swept the classroom. There was no water in the school building, so buckets were filled and carried in from a well that had been dug outside. The bathroom was in a little building outside, and it too had to be cleaned daily.

Children loved recess. They played tag and hide and seek. Often a big tree was in the schoolyard with a swing hanging from a branch. The children had great imaginations and made up games using rocks or marbles. Sometimes the boys sat on the steps or leaned against the fence and whittled on a stick. They made little boats and various animals. They knew that when they went back into the building they would have to work hard again.

A school bell summoned the children into the classroom. It was an honor to be chosen to ring that bell. The children brought lunches from home and enjoyed eating their meals outside when the weather permitted.

Each member of a village was important, even the children. They depended on each other. Students seldom had homework, because they had to help at home.

Facing page: Children often had to help their parents work in the fields.

CHAPTER 6

THE COLONIAL HOME

Most of the homes of the 18th century were very simple. They were often two stories high and usually had some sort of cellar. The cellar was important because it kept fruits and vegetables at a steady cool temperature. A big fireplace provided warmth and was often used for cooking. Benches were placed around the fireplace, since it was the center of home activities.

Homes were made of wood or stone. Southern plantation homes were larger. They were beautiful, and staffed by servants called slaves. Northern homes were sealed well to keep the winter winds from blowing through the cracks.

The colonists were up at dawn to begin their work. They went to bed at sundown. Homemade blankets and bonnets kept children warm at night. In the winter, bricks were heated and put under the covers to make the bed warm. Sometimes log cabins had holes between the logs. Children often woke in the morning to find snow on their quilts.

Baths were not taken very often. However, sometimes a big tub was filled with heated water, and each member of the family took turns bathing in the same water.

Swimming was a favorite summer activity. Children loved to go to the creek and jump in, especially when the weather was hot and humid. They often chose a place where a tree branch hung over the water. Then they draped a heavy rope over the branch and used it to swing out to the deeper water. They enjoyed dangling in midair and then making a big splash.

Soap making was usually done in the autumn. Rainwater was collected and used all through the year. But when it was time to make soap, it was held just for that purpose. Letting water seep through fireplace ashes made lye. Then the lye was boiled with melted fat or tallow and mixed with salt. Various fragrances could be added. Cleaning agents like borax were added to the laundry soap. Finally, the mixture was poured into big wooden boxes so it could harden overnight. Then it was cut and stored.

Soap was usually made after butchering because the animal fat was abundant. It was a smelly job and not one the women enjoyed, but one they had to do. The lye could be dangerous if it touched the skin, so children did not often help with soap making.

A house and garden in Colonial Williamsburg, Virginia.

Chapter 7

The Peddlers

Peddlers were important to the families. They traveled from town to town selling all kinds of things. Colonists could buy ribbon, cloth, pins and needles, toys, and other novelties. Sometimes they had pots and pans, too. Peddlers usually made so much noise bumping along the road that the entire family would stand waiting for their arrival. The ladies wanted to see all the new gadgets.

Often peddlers had news to share, and the men were anxious to learn of recent happenings in other villages. The peddlers usually traveled a regular route, called a circuit, and stopped at most of the homes along the way.

Candles could be purchased from the peddlers, too. However, most women made their own. It was necessary to have a good supply of candles. They provided light for the home. Candles were usually made in the autumn after the butchering was done. The fat became tallow for the candles. Various scents were added to make the air pleasant and fragrant.

Left: A girl in traditional clothing demonstrates how to make candles. *Facing page:* A vegetable peddler.

CHAPTER 8

COMMUNITY LIFE

Quilting bees were common in the homes of the colonists. They were held to make bed covers called quilts. Every home had several quilts. However, quilting bees were considered a good social time. They were planned especially for couples who were to be married. Ladies met in the home of the bride and stitched on the same quilt. They sewed together two pieces of material with a soft substance between the layers. Ladies took great pride in being able to make tiny stitches. Quilts were always a treasured gift for the bride and groom.

The people in homes and villages worked together. They helped each other. If a fire or flood occurred, they gave food and shelter. They knew that their success often depended on each other.

Quilting bees were an opportunity for colonists to socialize.

Fiddlers were in high demand at barn dances, where colonists came to socialize and dance to the music.

People also played together. Barn dances were held on Saturday nights. There was usually someone in the village who played the fiddle. The people gathered together and listened to the music and square danced.

Occasionally there would be a big party. Ladies would put on their pretty gowns. Men often wore white powdered wigs to parties. They would dance and listen to music. However, these parties were usually held in the big cities. People who lived in small towns and villages settled for the barn dances.

Horseshoes was a game that men loved to play. Two posts were placed in the ground about 40 feet (12.2 m) apart. Players tossed the horseshoe to the stake at the other end. Points were awarded for circling or being the nearest to the stake.

Most farmers raised their own meat, usually pork and chicken. Pigs were killed in the cold weather. The hams were hung in the smokehouse. Sausage and bacon was smoked. Meat was also canned. Chickens were killed as needed, often for the Sunday dinner.

CHAPTER 9

FOOD OF THE COLONISTS

Hunting was a sport that put food on the table. Deer, ducks, geese, wild turkey, squirrel, and rabbits were used for meat. Boys were taught how to shoot guns by age 10.

Every family had a garden. They worked hard to make sure it produced vegetables that could be stored for winter use.

Colonists enjoyed sauerkraut, which was made in the autumn. Cabbage was cut and put into a big crock and seasoned with salt. It was then placed in the cellar for about a month before serving. Children loved to sneak into the cellar and dip out a little kraut.

Wild bird shooters crouch with their dogs on a lakeshore.

A woman shows a plate of prepared greens at a re-created settlement at Plymouth, Massachusetts.

Bread and butter were made about once a week. Butter was made in a churn. Cream was saved throughout the week and then poured into the churn. It was stirred with a big paddle for up to four hours. The liquid taken off was called buttermilk, and the remaining lump was butter. Several loaves of bread and pounds of butter were made to serve the family each week. The extra butter was taken to the general store and traded.

In the spring, maple trees were tapped so that the sap would run into an attached can. The sap was boiled down and became maple syrup.

CHAPTER 10

CHORES

Every family member had a number of jobs to do. These were called chores. Girls gathered eggs. They also helped make clothing, repair socks, and make candles. They learned to do various kinds of stitchery, like embroidery or knitting. One of their most important jobs was watching their little brothers and sisters. They also helped keep the garden free of weeds.

Boys carried water from the spring or stream. They milked the cows and fed the pigs. They chopped wood and learned how to put a yoke on the oxen so crops could be worked and planted. Boys helped their fathers in the fields, too. Seed was spread by hand, and so was some of the harvesting. Wheat was thrashed by hand so it could be

Inside a Colonial kitchen.

ground into flour. Flax was an important crop in some of the Colonies. It was used for making linen clothes.

Boys also helped build fences. These were constructed from cut trees and put together by making notches so that the logs fit together. Fence building and repairing was a never-ending job.

Even little children helped in the Colonial home. They looked after the smaller animals. When the berries were ripe, they picked them for pies. They enjoyed this job. They could sing, talk, and eat all the berries they wanted.

A horse-drawn carriage in Colonial Williamsburg.

A job that sometimes fell to teenage boys was that of taming wild horses. A farmer had to have good teams to work in the fields. Good horses were important to families because they provided transportation. Families rode in buggies pulled by horses. Their horses had names and were well taken care of. Farmers often had mules or oxen as well.

Herbs were important to the colonists. They always planted a section of their garden with herbs. These were used not only for food seasoning, but also for medicines. Doctors did not know how to treat many diseases. Various herbs often made a patient feel better.

Instead of a patient going to the doctor's office, the doctor often went to the home. This was called a house call. Babies were usually born at home. There were some hospitals in the larger cities, but most medical care was given in the home. There were no dentists.

Many babies died before they were five years old, especially if they were not strong. Sometimes women died in childbirth. The doctors and people did not know the importance of cleanliness. They did not know how to treat many diseases.

CHAPTER 11

CONCLUSION

It was not an easy life for many of the colonists, but they enjoyed their homes and families. They worked and played together. They took time to read the Bible and worship together. They needed each other. They shared their good news as well as their sad times. Because their lives were so intertwined, they depended upon each other.

Knowing this helps us understand how disturbed they were when the British came to America with plans to change the system and impose heavy taxes. The colonists were self-supporting and doing quite well. They wanted to keep it that way. They enjoyed being a part of England as long as England stayed away. Interference by the British would only mean trouble for the colonists. In turn, trouble for the colonists meant trouble for England.

In the end, one question was asked: Would England leave the Colonies alone, or would the Colonies be forced to revolt and declare themselves independent of the Mother Country of England?

A woman taking down the American flag at Colonial Williamsburg, Virginia.

INTERNET SITES

ushistory.org
http://www.ushistory.org/

This Internet exploration of the Revolutionary War is presented by the Independence Hall Association. Visitors can learn interesting facts about many aspects of the war, including major battles, biographies of important patriots (Ben Franklin, Betsy Ross, Thomas Paine, and others), plus information on historic sites that can be toured today. The section on the Declaration of Independence includes photos of the document, as well as biographies of the signers and Jefferson's account of the writing.

Liberty! The American Revolution
http://www.pbs.org/ktca/liberty/

The official online companion to "Liberty! The American Revolution," a series of documentaries originally broadcast on PBS in 1997. Includes timelines, resource material, and related topics—a potpourri of information on the American Revolution. Topics cover daily life in the colonies, the global village, a military point of view, plus a section on the making of the TV series. Also includes a "Revolutionary Game."

These sites are subject to change. Go to your favorite search engine and type in "American Revolution" for more sites.

PASS IT ON

American Revolutionary War buffs: educate readers around the country by passing on interesting information you've learned about the American Revolution. Maybe your family visited a famous Revolutionary War battle site, or you've taken part in a reenactment. Who's your favorite historical figure from the Revolutionary War? We want to hear from you!

To get posted on the ABDO Publishing Company Web site, email us at "History@abdopub.com"

Visit the ABDO Publishing Company Web site at www.abdopub.com

GLOSSARY

Anvil

A block which is used by a blacksmith to form metal.

Apprentice

Usually a young person learning a craft or trade under the watchful eye of a skilled worker.

Barn Dance

A social event usually held in someone's barn on Saturday night.

Butcher

One who kills the farm animals used for food. The butcher shop was the place where they were killed and sold to customers.

Cellar

An area usually under the house where food could be put and kept at an even temperature. It could also be dug into a hillside.

Churn

A container that sits on the floor and has a tall paddle used to stir cream until it turns into butter.

Circuit

A regular route traveled by the lawyers, judges, preachers, peddlers, and the post rider.

Colony

A group of people who settle in a distant territory but remain citizens of their native country.

Hornbook

A wooden paddle with an attached piece of paper which listed the alphabet and numbers.

Horseshoes

Metal plates made by the blacksmith to protect the feet of horses. It was also a game where old horseshoes were tossed at stakes 40 feet apart.

Lye

Rainwater that has seeped through ashes and is used to make soap.

Miller

A person who grounds the wheat and corn into flour and cornmeal.

Peddler

One who traveled on a circuit and sold all kinds of items to the colonists.

Plantations

Very large farms located in the South.

Quilt

A blanket made by sewing small pieces of cloth together. Some sort of soft material was placed between two layers and then sewn together with tiny stitches. There was usually a pattern in the positioning of the pieces of cloth.

Skilled Craftsman

A person who had a special skill or ability and had been trained in a certain job.

Slate Board

Small blackboards held by hand and used by the students to do their studies.

Smokehouse

A small building where ham, bacon, and sausage were hung. A hickory wood fire was kept smoking for several days, preserving the meat and giving it a distinct flavor.

Tallow

A solid substance that was made from melted and mixed animal fats and used to make soap and candles.

Town Crier

A person who sang the latest news on the street corners of the village.

INDEX

7/02